The Enjoyment of Christ for the Body in 1 Corinthians

WITNESS LEE

Living Stream Ministry
Anaheim, CA • www.lsm.org

First Edition, November 2005.

ISBN 0-7363-3019-4

Published by

Living Stream Ministry
2431 W. La Palma Ave., Anaheim, CA 92801 U.S.A.
P. O. Box 2121, Anaheim, CA 92814 U.S.A.

Printed in the United States of America

05 06 07 08 09 10 11 / 9 8 7 6 5 4 3 2 1

CONTENTS

PREFACE

This book is composed of messages given by Brother Witness Lee in March and April 1973, in Houston, Texas.

CHAPTER ONE

ENJOYING CHRIST PRACTICALLY AS THE LIFE-GIVING SPIRIT TO BE ONE SPIRIT WITH HIM

Scripture Reading: 1 Cor. 1:2, 9, 13a, 22-24, 30; 2:1-2, 7, 9-12, 14-15; 15:45b; 12:13, 3b; 6:17; 7:40b

As the first of the New Testament Epistles, the book of Romans is a sketch of the Christian life and the church life. Romans is followed by 1 Corinthians, which reveals some truly wonderful items. If we consider the expositions of the New Testament throughout the centuries, we can realize that the depths, mysteries, and hidden things in 1 Corinthians have been discovered, or recovered, only in recent years. Knowing the hidden depths in 1 Corinthians can be compared to knowing the mystery of the universe and knowing the mystery within man. The universe is composed of the heavens, the earth, and many items. It is easy to see the physical things in the universe; however, it is not easy to realize what the depth, mystery, and kernel of the universe are. We may say that the mystery of the universe is Jesus, but to apply this and make it even more practical, it is better to say that the mystery of the universe is the divine Spirit.

Just as the mystery of the universe is the divine Spirit, the mystery within man is the human spirit. When we look at a person, we see his physical body, but the mystery within this physical body is the human spirit (Job 32:8a; Prov. 20:27; 1 Cor. 2:11a; 1 Thes. 5:23). Atheists say that there is no divine Spirit in the universe, and many people also say that there is no spirit within man. However, without the divine Spirit, the universe would be a lifeless thing, and without the human spirit, the body would be a corpse. The entire universe depends on the divine Spirit, and a human being depends on the human spirit. It is easy to see all the outward things without seeing that the divine Spirit is the mystery of the universe and that our human spirit is the mystery of our human being. In the same way, it is easy to see many items in 1 Corinthians without touching the depths and the mysteries within this book.

First Corinthians speaks of many matters, such as lawsuits among believers (6:1-11), marriage life (7:1-40), the Lord's table (10:14-22), head covering (11:2-16), and speaking in tongues (12:10, 28). Many Christians magnify chapter 12 because speaking in tongues is mentioned there. When a member of our body keeps its appropriate size, it remains normal and performs its function for the benefit of the body. However, if a member is enlarged out of proportion, it becomes abnormal, it places a heavy burden on the body, and it loses its function. God's design of our body can never be improved upon; thus, every part should remain in its proper size and proportion. Likewise, chapter 12 is only one of sixteen chapters in 1 Corinthians. Speaking in tongues is mentioned in chapter 12, but it must be kept in its proper proportion, as Paul points out in chapter 14. Strictly speaking, the subject of 1 Corinthians is neither marriage nor head covering nor tongue-speaking. It is easy to see the outward matters in 1 Corinthians, but it is difficult to find the depths, the mystery, in this book. This is the reason that from the time of the Reformation until the present century, this book was never opened up in its depths. Only in the last few years has this book been open to us.

THE CHURCH OF GOD
BEING IN A LOCALITY PRACTICALLY

Each book in the Bible begins in a specific way. Genesis, Exodus, Matthew, and John all begin differently, according to their specific purpose. Paul begins 1 Corinthians by addressing his Epistle to "the church of God which is in Corinth" (1:2a). This Epistle is written to the church of God in the locality of Corinth. Some people have condemned the teaching that the church is expressed in each locality. They say that the church is heavenly, and to bring it down to a locality makes it earthly. However, Paul begins this Epistle by addressing the church of God which is in Corinth. To say that the church is heavenly is to speak in a doctrinal way, but to speak of the church in a certain locality is to be practical. The church in a locality is the church in practicality. If there is no practical church in our locality, we should endeavor to gather a few saints together to become the church, but if we cannot do this, we may need to move to a locality where there is a local church. No one can live properly without a home and a family. If anyone does not have a family, he is a wanderer. In the same way, we, as Christians, cannot live without the church expressed in a practical way in our locality. It is too doctrinal to speak of the church in the heavens. We need to be practical.

CALLING ON THE NAME OF OUR LORD JESUS CHRIST

In verse 2 Paul also mentions "all those who call upon the name of our Lord Jesus Christ." In this verse Paul does not address his Epistle to those who merely study the Bible, pray in their homes, or speak in tongues. Rather, he addresses it to all those who call on the name of the Lord. Paul had a particular purpose in writing in this way. Genesis begins with, "In the beginning God created the heavens and the earth" (1:1), because this book goes on to speak of God's creation. Likewise, the Gospel of John opens with, "In the beginning was the Word, and the Word was with God, and the Word was God" (1:1), because John tells us that Christ is eternal. In the same way, the beginning of 1 Corinthians tells us that it is a book that deals with calling on the name of the Lord. Many people have read, studied, and researched 1 Corinthians, but their eyes were not open to see the matter of calling on the name of the Lord. In order to properly partake of this book, we must be in a church that is not in the heavens but in our locality, and we must also call, "O Lord Jesus."

Some may say that to call on the name of the Lord is a form or a regulation. To be sure, we need to drop many forms and regulations, but there are certain "regulations" that we must never drop, such as breathing, drinking, and eating. We can drop the form of sitting in pews, but we should never give up calling on the Lord. To drop our calling on the Lord is to drop our spiritual breathing, drinking, and eating. Others have said that people will not receive our practice of calling on the Lord, but many thousands have already received help by calling in this way. Calling on the Lord makes a great difference in our experience. Those who call on the name of the Lord are more living than those who remain silent. Some may also argue that calling on the Lord is not orderly. A certain short history of the Welsh revival of 1904 and 1905 records that many hundreds of people at that time shouted in their enjoyment of the Lord. According to this account, some people criticized this practice as being excessive. However, many people go to football games to shout. Is Jesus not more worthy of our shouting?

Some have argued that this kind of shouting is not found in the Bible, but we have found that to shout to the Lord is very scriptural. When the Lord entered Jerusalem for the last time, many of the people spread their own garments in the road and went before the Lord, rejoicing and praising God with a loud voice, saying, "Hosanna to the Son of David!" and "Blessed is the King who comes in the name of the Lord!" When the religious Pharisees, the chief priests, and the scribes saw these things, they were indignant and told the Lord, "Rebuke Your disciples." Instead, the Lord Jesus said, "If these shall be silent, the stones will cry out" (Matt. 21:8-9, 15; Luke 19:37-40). In our own homes we may simply sit or kneel and call, "O Lord Jesus! Lord Jesus!" Whoever calls on the name of the Lord will see that it makes a difference in his experience. The Lord is rich to all who call upon Him (Rom. 10:12).

To call on the name of the Lord is not merely to pray. When we call, we are praying, but according to the meaning of the Greek word, to call is to shout, to cry loudly. There is nothing wrong with silent prayer, but there may be little enjoyment in it. When we change our prayer into calling, we have both prayer and enjoyment. Many times we may not need to pray in a common way; we may simply need to enjoy the Lord. If we are having a difficult time with our wife, for example, we should not pray that the Lord will change her.

Rather, we simply need to call, "O Lord Jesus!" Our enjoying the Lord in this way will transform us.

First Corinthians 1:2 speaks of calling on the name of "our Lord Jesus Christ...who is theirs and ours." Nowhere else in the New Testament can we find such an expression. We need to call on the Lord Jesus because He is our portion (Col. 1:12). He is Paul's portion, Peter's portion, and our portion for us to enjoy. First Corinthians 1:9 says, "God is faithful, through whom you were called into the fellowship of His Son, Jesus Christ our Lord." *Fellowship* here indicates participation. God has called us all into the enjoyment of and participation in Jesus Christ, who is our portion. Later in the chapter, verse 13 asks, "Is Christ divided?" Jesus Christ is not divided. When we all enjoy Christ, we are one because the very Christ whom we enjoy is one. This oneness in the enjoyment of Christ our portion is the proper church life.

THE CRUCIFIED AND RESURRECTED CHRIST BEING GOD'S WISDOM AND GOD'S POWER TO US

Verse 22 says, "Indeed Jews require signs and Greeks seek wisdom." A sign is a miraculous token given to substantiate what is preached. For Balaam's donkey to speak in a human language was a sign (Num. 22:28-30). In principle, all the miraculous gifts, such as speaking in tongues, are signs. The Jews continually required miraculous signs. When the Lord Jesus was on the earth, some of the scribes and Pharisees said to Him, "Teacher, we want to see a sign from You." The Lord Jesus said, "An evil and adulterous generation seeks after a sign, and a sign shall not be given to it except the sign of Jonah the prophet. For just as Jonah was in the belly of the great fish three days and three nights, so will the Son of Man be in the heart of the earth three days and three nights" (Matt. 12:38-40). The sign given to us today is not something miraculous; it is the crucified and resurrected Christ.

The Greeks, on the other hand, seek wisdom, that is, knowledge, doctrine, and teaching. First Corinthians not only speaks of spiritual gifts, but it also has a certain amount of teaching concerning marriage life, head covering, the Lord's table, and other matters. In principle, the expositions of the

Brethren teachers in the nineteenth and twentieth centuries mainly follow the Greeks to emphasize the teachings in this book, and the Pentecostal teachings mostly follow the Jews to emphasize the gifts. However, Paul says, "We preach Christ crucified, to Jews a stumbling block, and to Gentiles foolishness" (1:23). We do not care for signs, gifts, doctrines, or teachings. We are neither Jews nor Greeks but partakers of Christ. Moreover, to the called ones, Christ is the power of God and the wisdom of God (v. 24). Verse 30 says, "Of Him you are in Christ Jesus, who became wisdom to us from God: both righteousness and sanctification and redemption." Christ is everything to us. He is God's power and God's wisdom as our righteousness for the past, our sanctification for the present, and our redemption for the future.

CHRIST REVEALED TO US BY THE DIVINE SPIRIT IN OUR HUMAN SPIRIT

Verses 1 and 2 of chapter 2 say, "I, when I came to you, brothers, came not according to excellence of speech or of wisdom, announcing to you the mystery of God. For I did not determine to know anything among you except Jesus Christ, and this One crucified." In verse 7 Paul goes on to say, "But we speak God's wisdom in a mystery." The wisdom Paul preached is Christ as our wisdom, as mentioned in 1:30. Eye has not seen and ear has not heard the deep and hidden things pertaining to Christ as God's wisdom, nor have these things come up in man's heart, but God has prepared them for those who love Him and has revealed them by means of the two spirits, the divine Spirit and the human spirit (2:9-12). God reveals Christ to us through these two spirits. If we do not care for the two spirits, we are soulish men, men who live in the soul. God requires us to forsake our soul and turn to our spirit so that we may be spiritual men, those who live, walk, and do things in their spirit (vv. 14-15). It is in the regenerated spirit of man that God the Spirit dwells (Rom. 8:9, 11, 16).

CHRIST BECOMING THE LIFE-GIVING SPIRIT TO BE WHAT WE NEED IN A PRACTICAL WAY

First Corinthians 15:45b says, "The last Adam became a

life-giving Spirit." Without Christ becoming the life-giving Spirit, all that is taught in chapters 1 and 2 is mere doctrinal knowledge to us. To know that food is nourishing means nothing in itself. We need to apply this knowledge by eating the food. Similarly, in order for Christ to be our power, wisdom, righteousness, sanctification, and redemption, we must see that today Christ is the life-giving Spirit. If He were not the Spirit, He could not be these things to us. He and we would be separate persons and could have nothing to do with one another in a practical way. Today Christ is the life-giving Spirit to be all the aforementioned items to us. Whenever we call on His name, the life-giving Spirit comes into us. When we need righteousness, victory, power, or light, He becomes all these things to us in a practical way. We may know that Christ is our patience and love, but this may only be a doctrine to us. We must realize that He is now the life-giving Spirit and apply Him in a practical way by calling, "O Lord Jesus." Whenever a brother is bothered by his roommate, he can remind himself in a doctrinal way that Christ is his patience, but eventually his natural patience will be exhausted. This is because he has the doctrine that Christ is his patience, but he does not experience Christ as his patience. Whenever he is bothered, he should call, "O Lord Jesus!" Then he will have not merely the doctrine but the experience of Christ as his patience.

Doctrine without practical application means little. We need to apply the Lord Jesus to our situation. We can realize the way to apply the Lord Jesus by considering the whole of 1 Corinthians. Chapter 1 speaks of calling on the name of the Lord, who is the portion of all the believers. We have been called into the enjoyment of Christ as our portion, and this Christ is wisdom to us from God: both righteousness and sanctification and redemption. Then chapter 2 tells us that this portion can be realized by us only in our spirit. Moreover, chapter 15 tells us that Christ as our portion is now the life-giving Spirit. If Christ were not the life-giving Spirit but were only far away in the third heaven, we could not receive Him. Today, however, our Lord Jesus is the life-giving Spirit to be real, living, near, and available to us. Therefore, whenever we call on the name of Jesus, He comes to us immediately, and we receive His person. Jesus is His name, and the life-giving Spirit is His person. Therefore, day by day we all need to call, "O Lord Jesus." When we call on this dear name, we receive His precious person as the life-giving Spirit. Then He becomes whatever we need. If we need righteousness, He is our righteousness. If we need sanctification, He is our sanctification. If we need submission, when we call on the name of the Lord Jesus, He comes as the life-giving Spirit to be our submission.

Many times I become weak by the end of the afternoon, because the nourishment I received in the morning and at noontime has been exhausted. However, shortly after supper I am strengthened and invigorated again, not by the doctrine of nourishment but by my practical eating, by my taking food into me. The food we eat is our supply of energy and strength. The tragedy of today's Christianity is that people have many doctrinal teachings with little practical application. In His recovery, the Lord is turning us, causing us not to care for mere doctrines but simply to call on the name of the Lord Jesus, who is the life-giving Spirit. If we have a problem with someone, we should not try to apply a doctrine to our situation. This will not work. We simply need to call, "O Lord Jesus." Then we will receive the living person of Jesus as the life-giving Spirit, the Spirit who ministers life to us.

We must all see that Jesus is not a mere doctrine. Jesus is real, living, near, and available. A person may be real, but if he is not living and near, he cannot come when we call him. Likewise, if he does not care for us and is not available to us, he will not come when we call. However, the Lord Jesus is not like this. On the contrary, He is real. There is nothing as real as Jesus. He is also living, and He is near, even in our mouth (Rom. 10:8). No one but Jesus can be as near as this. Moreover, He is available. Because of this, whenever we call on Him, He comes into us. Some persons have called on Jesus without a full sincerity or intention to receive Him; nevertheless, simply by calling, they were captured by Him. The Lord Jesus is always real, living, near, and available to us regardless of our sincerity in calling on Him. If someone is not a Christian, he can still come to Jesus, saying, "Jesus, I do not believe

in You, and I do not love You." Jesus may gradually say to such
a person, "You do not love Me, but I love you." We have seen
some persons be saved in this way. Jesus is not a doctrine; He
is a living person, the life-giving Spirit. In my early years as a
believer, I received the knowledge of the Bible at the feet of
the Brethren for several years, but one day I realized that
I was void of life. At that time I cried out to the Lord, and by
crying out in this way, I received life.

BEING IN CHRIST BY BEING BAPTIZED IN ONE SPIRIT

First Corinthians 1:30 says, "Of Him you are in Christ
Jesus." When we believe in Jesus, receiving Him by calling on
His name, He comes into us as the life-giving Spirit. From
that time on, we cannot get away from Him, because we have
been put into Him by God. To be put into Jesus is to be baptized in one Spirit. Verse 13 of chapter 12 begins, "For also in
one Spirit we were all baptized into one Body." The one Spirit
in chapter 12 is the life-giving Spirit in chapter 15. Some
people ask, "Have you been baptized in the Holy Spirit?"
Many Christians dare not answer positively, supposing that
since they have not spoken in tongues, they have not been
baptized in the Spirit. This is a wrong concept. According to
1 Corinthians 1:30, we believers are all in Christ, and according to 15:45, Christ is the life-giving Spirit. Therefore, we are
in the Spirit. This indicates that we have all been baptized in
the Spirit. This is truly scriptural and logical. From now on, if
anyone asks if we have been baptized in the Spirit, we should
say, "I am in Christ. Therefore, I am in the life-giving Spirit."
In Greek, *were all baptized* in 12:13 is in the aorist tense,
indicating that our baptism in the Spirit has been accomplished. We have all been baptized in one Spirit.

DRINKING THE ONE SPIRIT
TO BE ONE SPIRIT WITH THE LORD

Verse 13 continues, "And were all given to drink one Spirit."
We are in Christ, but now we need to take Christ into us. To
be baptized is to be put into water, but to drink is to take the
water into us. Many in Christianity pay attention to baptism,
but they neglect drinking. Our baptism in the Spirit has been

accomplished, but our drinking the Spirit is ongoing. Through baptism we have been positioned to drink the Spirit; therefore, now we need to drink all day long. Verse 3 shows the way to drink. This verse says, "No one can say, Jesus is Lord! except in the Holy Spirit." Whenever we say, "Lord Jesus!" we are in the Spirit, and we are drinking the one Spirit. By drinking the Spirit, we become one spirit with the Lord Jesus (6:17). He is the life-giving Spirit, and we have all been put into Him and have been positioned to drink of Him day by day. We are in Him, and He is in us; hence, we are one with Him. We are in the Spirit, and we are drinking the Spirit. As a result, the Spirit is in us, and we are one spirit with the Lord. In this one spirit we experience Christ as our light, life, power, holiness, sanctification, and everything. In this spirit we also have the church life. If we truly see this, we will be beside ourselves.

We should not count on our feelings as proof that we have been baptized in the Spirit. Our feelings can be very deceptive. After speaking for an entire chapter concerning marriage life, Paul said, "I think that I also have the Spirit of God" (7:40). It seems that he did not have much assurance. Someone might have said to him, "Brother Paul, if you do not have the assurance that you have the Spirit, you should not say anything." Nevertheless, what he said in chapter 7 is the word of the Bible today. Because Paul was a person who lived in the mingled spirit—the human spirit mingled with the divine Spirit—whatever he said was God's word, even though he did not have a strong feeling about it. This illustrates that we should not care for our feelings. We must care only for the facts and the practicality. The fact is that we were all baptized into Christ, who is the life-giving Spirit. When we believed in Him and called on His name, we entered into Him, and He entered into us. Now we all need to take this fact and call on His name hour after hour. We may compare calling to breathing. We are in the air around us, but by our breathing, the air enters into us. On the one hand, we are in the air, and on the other hand, the air is in us. Eventually, we become one with the air. Likewise, our breathing the Lord Jesus as the life-giving Spirit makes us one spirit with Him. By our breathing and drinking the one Spirit, He comes into us more and more. As a result, whatever we do and say is something of the Lord. Like Paul, we can say, "I think that I also have the Spirit of God." This kind of experience is the proper Christian life that issues in the church life.

CHAPTER TWO

EATING AND DRINKING CHRIST
IN 1 CORINTHIANS

Scripture Reading: 1 Cor. 3:2a, 6, 9b, 11-12a; 5:7b-8a; 10:3-4, 16-17, 21; 11:23-26; 12:13b; 15:20; Rev. 22:14, 17

At the beginning of the Bible there is the tree of life for man's eating, and there is also a river that signifies the river of water of life (Gen. 2:9-10, 16; Rev. 22:1-2). In the New Testament the Lord Jesus told His disciples that they needed to eat Him and drink Him (John 6:35, 48, 51, 54, 57; 4:14; 7:37-39). In the second of the Epistles, the book of 1 Corinthians, there are a number of verses related to eating and drinking. Throughout the past centuries the matters of eating and drinking the Lord have never been as clear in this book as they are today. Many expositions of 1 Corinthians say almost nothing about eating and drinking the Lord. Instead, they speak concerning teachings and spiritual gifts, especially the gift of speaking in tongues. However, the verses in this book concerning eating and drinking are strong and strategic. When we read them, we can sense Paul's particular tone and utterance.

As we saw in the previous message, 1 Corinthians 1 tells us that the believers in Christ are those who call on the name of the Lord. According to this chapter, we are the called saints, and God has called us into the fellowship of His Son. In addition, we are those who call on the name of our Lord Jesus Christ (vv. 2, 9). This is a two-way calling. First, God called us, and now we call on the Lord Jesus. We have not been called by God to be dumb; we have been called to call. We are the called ones and the calling ones. To call on the name of the Lord is to participate in Him as our allotted portion. Christ as our portion is the power of God and the wisdom of God as righteousness for our past (vv. 24, 30). Since our past was so miserable, we need the Lord Jesus to be our righteousness so that we may be justified by God. Christ as the wisdom of God is also sanctification for our present and redemption for our future. He is everything to us in relation to the three stages of time. Christ as our portion is fully adequate to meet our need.

Then chapter 2 tells us how to participate in Christ as our portion. We need to realize that our portion today is the divine Spirit in our spirit. Therefore, we must live in our spirit as spiritual men, not in our soul as soulish men (vv. 10-15). A soulish man relies on his mind to think and to meditate. This is to use the wrong organ to contact the Lord. We need to stop our mentality and turn to our spirit, where Jesus is (2 Tim. 4:22). This is the way to touch the Lord Jesus as the life-giving Spirit in our spirit (1 Cor. 15:45b; 2 Cor. 3:17; Rom. 8:16). It is not adequate for us simply to make up our mind to turn to our spirit. The more we do this, the more we will remain in our mind and our will, which are parts of our soul. Moreover, the more we remain in our soul, the more soulish we will be. The best way to turn to our spirit to meet the divine Spirit as our portion for our enjoyment is to call, "O Lord Jesus!"

It is not sufficient for us to simply talk about the need to exercise our feet. If this is all we do, our feet will eventually be out of function. The way to exercise our feet is either to walk, run, or jump. Likewise, the most prevailing way to exercise our spirit is to call on the name of the Lord. If a person receives only the teaching concerning the exercise of the spirit, one day when someone bothers him, he may think, "I was told that this is the time to turn to my spirit. Now I should do it." Eventually, however, he may forget the teaching and speak a harsh word to that person. To merely have a teaching without applying it is the wrong way. When we are troubled by something, we need to stop the exercise of our mind and say, "O Lord Jesus. Praise the Lord! Amen." This is the best way to turn to our spirit.

BEING FED WITH CHRIST FOR THE GROWTH IN LIFE

In 1 Corinthians 3:2 Paul says, "I gave you milk to drink,"

and in verse 6 he says, "I planted, Apollos watered, but God caused the growth." All mothers know that the way to help their children grow is not by teaching them. The only way for a child to grow is for someone to feed him. Paul planted something in the Corinthians, and Apollos followed to water what Paul had planted. Then God honored the planting and the watering by causing the growth. Feeding brings in growth. This is why we do not like to follow Christianity in the way of emphasizing teachings. Rather, we prefer to follow the apostle Paul to feed the saints, to minister food and nourishment to the brothers and sisters so that they may grow. In the past years we have seen the saints grow day by day and year after year. In the local churches the saints are always growing. I do not like to criticize anyone, but I must speak the facts. I was in Christianity for many years, and I observed that people remained the same year after year. Some attend Sunday school every Sunday morning and remain under certain teachings for many years, but they do not have any growth. However, attending even one meeting in the local churches causes us to be different.

EATING CHRIST AS THE PASSOVER FEAST

The only way to grow is by eating. Paul tells us that Christ is our Passover (5:7b-8a). When many Christians speak of the Passover, they emphasize the applying of the blood (Exo. 12:7, 13). Few ever speak of the enjoyment of the passover feast. To the children of Israel, the Passover was a great enjoyment. They not only put the blood on the doorposts, but they also ate the lamb with unleavened bread and bitter herbs (v. 8). This is why Paul says, "Let us keep the feast" (1 Cor. 5:8). He did not tell us to keep the ritual, the commandment, or the teaching; he told us to keep the feast. The Christian life and the church life are a feast that we keep every day. When many of us were in Christianity, we kept the fast, not the feast, because there was nothing there to eat, but in the church life we keep the feast. I have been on the way of the church life for over forty years, and it has always been a feast to me. Some have criticized us for being beside ourselves in our enjoyment. To be sure, we are beside ourselves in our church feast (2 Cor. 5:13). After meeting with the saints, we are all joyful and filled.

EATING CHRIST AS OUR SPIRITUAL FOOD AND DRINKING HIM AS OUR SPIRITUAL DRINK

First Corinthians 10:3 and 4 say, "All ate the same spiritual food, and all drank the same spiritual drink; for they drank of a spiritual rock which followed them, and the rock was Christ." Certain hymns in Christianity refer to Christ being the rock mainly as the solid foundation for our redemption. However, in 1 Corinthians 10 Christ as the rock is not mainly for our redemption but for our drinking and enjoyment. We all need to eat the same spiritual food and drink the same spiritual drink by drinking of Christ as our rock.

EATING AND DRINKING THE LORD AT HIS TABLE TO BECOME HIS ONE BODY

In verses 16, 17, and 21 Paul speaks concerning the bread and the cup at the Lord's table. On His last night with the disciples, the Lord Jesus did not pick up the Scriptures and expound them, saying, "This is My teaching. Keep this in remembrance of Me." In principle, this is the way many in Christianity remember the Lord. Rather, the Lord took bread and a cup. Bread is good only for eating, and a cup is good only for drinking. The Lord said, "This do unto the remembrance of Me" (11:24; Luke 22:19). By *this* He was referring to eating the bread and drinking the cup. The best and unique way to remember the Lord Jesus is not to think, to meditate, or to recall but simply to eat and drink Him. The more we eat Jesus at His table, the more He is happy with us. He does not care to see us humble ourselves by kneeling or prostrating ourselves before Him. The Lord may say, "Foolish child, I do not care whether you kneel or not. I want to see you eat. The more you eat Me, the happier I am."

The more Christ enters into us, the more we remember Him. The best way to remember the Lord Jesus is not to worship and adore Him as the One who is high above in the third heaven. If we remember the Lord in that way, He may say to us, "Foolish ones, I am not only there in the heavens. I am here in your spirit. Simply enjoy Me. The more you eat and drink Me, the happier I am. I do not want to be above you; I want to be constituted into you. I do not want to be separate from you; I want to be one with you." The more we eat, the more the food is constituted into us. After every Lord's table we can tell the universe, including Satan, "Praise the Lord! We love Jesus, and now we have more of Him in us."

First Corinthians 10:21 refers to the Lord's table. The Lord's table is not a desk with a Bible for us to study. Rather, it is a table with two "main courses," the bread for eating and the cup for drinking. At the Lord's table we feast on the Lord, on His body and on His blood. This feasting issues in our being constituted to be one Body. Verse 17 says, "Seeing that there is one bread, we who are many are one Body; for we all partake of the one bread." The enjoyment of Christ brings forth the proper church life. If we come together only to exercise our mind, we will eventually stir up disputations in the mind. This will bring in resentment and fighting among us, and we will lose the oneness. Mere doctrinal teachings stir up differing opinions. Even a husband and wife may not be able to agree on certain teachings. It is impossible for us to be one merely by studying the Bible. Instead, the more we eat and drink of Jesus, the more we are one. The enjoyment of Jesus preserves us in oneness.

BEING POSITIONED IN ONE BODY
TO DRINK OF ONE SPIRIT

Verse 13 of chapter 12 says that we "were all given to drink one Spirit." We have been positioned to drink the Spirit. This position is in the one Body, the church. If we do not remain in the Body, we will be in the wrong position, and it will be difficult for us to drink. We need to keep the proper position by remaining in the Body. In the church we are drinking the Lord day by day.

PARTAKING OF CHRIST AS THE FIRSTFRUITS

In chapter 15, verse 20 says, "Now Christ has been raised from the dead, the firstfruits of those who have fallen asleep." The word *fruit* implies eating, indicating enjoyment. Fresh fruits, such as Washington apples, Florida grapefruit, and California oranges, are all for eating. In resurrection Christ became the life-giving Spirit for us to drink and the first-fruits for us to eat. Christ today is not merely a teacher; He is the firstfruits for us to partake of. Believers have read verse 20 for centuries, but very few have seen that the firstfruits are for eating. Most believers have considered that the word *firstfruits* in this verse refers only to Christ as the first One raised from the dead. Although Christ is the first in resurrection, the word *firstfruits* also indicates that the resurrected Christ is to be eaten by us for our enjoyment.

EATING AND DRINKING PRODUCING TRANSFORMATION FOR THE BUILDING UP OF THE CHURCH

All the foregoing points show us the eating and drinking of Jesus in the book of 1 Corinthians. Eating and drinking afford us not only the growth in life but also the transformation in life (3:11-12a). Transformation is not merely an outward correction. It is an inward change in which the supply of Christ as life brings a new element into us and discharges the old element. We are not only growing; we are also being transformed. A few years ago we were "muddy clay," but today we can see a certain amount of the element of precious stone within us. We should not be bothered if there is still more mud than stone in our being. After a short while, we will be more transformed, and more of the mud will become precious stone. Our transformation into precious stones is for God's building (v. 9b). Verses 11 and 12 say, "Another foundation no one is able to lay besides that which is laid, which is Jesus Christ. But if anyone builds upon the foundation gold, silver, precious stones." The foundation has already been laid, and now we can build upon it, not with wood, grass, or stubble but with gold, silver, and precious stones. Eating affords us the growth in life, growth brings in transformation, and transformation is for the building up of the church. We cannot build up a local church merely by teaching or organizing. The only way to build up the church is to feed the saints. We need to feed on Jesus every day. By so doing, we will grow, and by growing, we will be transformed. This will cause us to become a solid piece of precious material that is good for the building up of the church.

This is the reason that for many centuries the subtle enemy, Satan, has hidden the matter of eating and drinking the Lord from God's children. We praise the Lord that in these last days the Lord is recovering this matter. He is removing the veils of religion, our old background, our old doctrines, and our old concepts that we may know His economy. His way to dispense Himself into us is not by teaching but by our eating and drinking the Lord Jesus. As we saw in the previous message, the mystery and depths of 1 Corinthians are the two spirits, the divine Spirit and the human spirit. These two spirits are for our eating and drinking the Lord. We eat the Lord and drink the divine Spirit in our human spirit. Therefore, we all need to apply our human spirit by calling on the name of the Lord Jesus. To call on the Lord is to eat and drink of Him. This is the strategic point in 1 Corinthians.

A PROMISE OF EATING AND A CALL TO DRINK BEING THE CONCLUSION OF THE ENTIRE BIBLE

The entire Bible concludes with a promise and a call. The promise is that those who wash their robes may have the right to eat of the tree of life (Rev. 22:14). The call is in verse 17, which says, "The Spirit and the bride say, Come! And let him who hears say, Come! And let him who is thirsty come; let him who wills take the water of life freely." The promise of eating and the call to drink are the conclusion of the entire Bible. From the beginning to the end, the entire Bible reveals the matter of eating and drinking the Lord.

CHAPTER THREE

THE ENJOYMENT OF THE RICHES OF CHRIST ISSUING IN THE CORPORATE CHRIST, THE BODY-CHRIST

Scripture Reading: 1 Cor. 11:3a; 15:23, 47b, 45b; 12:11-14; 10:16b-17; 11:29; Eph. 4:4a

CALLING ON THE LORD BEING THE KEY TO THE ENJOYMENT OF CHRIST

Apparently, the first two of the Epistles, Romans and 1 Corinthians, are not closely related. However, if we get into the kernel, depth, and mystery of these two books, we will see that they are one. Romans is rich in doctrinal teachings. Every chapter of that Epistle contains a basic doctrine. The key to the book of Romans, however, is in chapter 10. After all the teachings of the preceding chapters, verses 6 and 7 say, "'Do not say in your heart, Who will ascend into heaven?' that is, to bring Christ down; or, 'Who will descend into the abyss?' that is, to bring Christ up from the dead." Christ has already come down from heaven in incarnation, and He has come up from the abyss in resurrection. We may ask, since Christ has come down from heaven and come up from the abyss, where is He? According to the Bible, there are three "stories" in the universe—heaven, the earth, and the abyss, which is under the earth (Phil. 2:10). Heaven is the highest story, the abyss is the lowest, and the earth is between these two. Since Christ has come down from heaven and come up from the abyss, we may say that Christ today is on the earth, but this is not specific enough. Today Christ is not only on the earth. As the living Word, He is also in our mouth (Rom. 10:8). Today we have not only the Christ who came down from heaven and came up from the abyss but also the Christ who is in our mouth.

Romans 10 goes on to tell us the way to participate in Christ's riches. Verses 12 and 13 say, "There is no distinction between Jew and Greek, for the same Lord is Lord of all and rich to all who call upon Him; for 'whoever calls upon the name of the Lord shall be saved.'" These verses do not tell us that Christ is rich to all who only study the Bible, pray all day, work for Him desperately, or fast regularly. Rather, Christ is rich to all who call upon His name. There is no more prevailing way to participate in and partake of His riches. We are not able to participate in the riches of Christ merely by studying the Bible. This can be compared to studying a recipe or a menu without eating the food itself. The way to partake of the riches of food is to eat. Likewise, the way to partake of the riches of Christ is to call on Him, saying, "O Lord Jesus!"

A husband and wife may decide to read John 1 together. Verse 1 says, "In the beginning was the Word, and the Word was with God, and the Word was God." After they read this verse, the husband may ask, "What is the beginning, and how could the Word be with God and also be God?" Then the wife may reply that it is too puzzling to understand. This is the way of traditional Bible studies, from which those who participate receive little more than vain, empty knowledge. To study the Bible in a traditional way is like studying a menu without eating the food. The proper way to partake of the riches of Christ in John 1:1 is not to study this verse in a traditional way but to pray over, that is, to pray-read, this verse. We may pray-read John 1:1 by saying, "O Lord Jesus! In the beginning. Amen. O Lord, in the beginning was the Word. Hallelujah! Was the Word. Amen, Lord Jesus!" Reading and praying in this way makes a great difference. This is because the Lord is rich to all who call upon Him. If we pray-read John 1:1 for five minutes, we will be on fire. We will be nourished, watered, and even flooded with the riches of Christ. The way to enjoy Christ's riches is to call on Him. The Lord is rich to all who call upon Him. This is the key to Romans, the first Epistle in the New Testament.

The opening words of 1 Corinthians continue the book of Romans. Verse 2 of chapter 1 refers to "all those who call upon the name of our Lord Jesus Christ in every place, who is theirs and ours." In Romans we have the key to partaking of Christ's riches, but we do not have any instructions on how to use the key. The instructions are in 1 Corinthians. When we use the key to open all the doors in this Epistle, we find the riches of Christ in chapter after chapter.

CHRIST BEING THE POWER OF GOD, THE WISDOM OF GOD, AND OUR RIGHTEOUSNESS, SANCTIFICATION, AND REDEMPTION

We have already seen a number of items of the riches of Christ in this Epistle. Chapter 1 contains five items: Christ as the power of God, the wisdom of God, righteousness for the past, sanctification for the present, and redemption for the future (vv. 24, 30). As human beings, we all have the three stages of the past, the present, and the future. We always need Christ as our righteousness for the past. Even for yesterday, we need Christ as our righteousness. Likewise, in every "today" we need Him as our sanctification, and we need Him as our redemption for the future. Christ's riches are in three aspects for each of the three stages of our existence.

CHRIST BEING THE DEEP THINGS OF GOD

In chapter 2 Christ is the deep things of God (vv. 7-10)—things which eye has not seen, ear has not heard, and which have not come up in man's heart. Nuclear science and the knowledge required to land men on the moon are all superficial. We have something deeper, the deep things of God, which are simply Christ. Whoever does not have Christ in him is shallow and superficial. Hallelujah, we have something hidden, mysterious, and deep within us! People may ask us, "What happened to you? Why you are so happy? Did you earn a high degree or get a better job? Did you win a prize or receive a gift?" We are happy because we have something that is very deep and mysterious—Christ as the deep things of God. This is the sixth item of the riches of Christ in 1 Corinthians.

CHRIST BEING THE UNIQUE FOUNDATION, OUR PASSOVER FEAST, AND OUR SPIRITUAL FOOD, SPIRITUAL DRINK, AND SPIRITUAL ROCK

Christ is also the unique foundation laid by God for the building of the church (3:10-11), our Passover feast for our enjoyment (5:7-8), and our spiritual food, spiritual drink, and spiritual rock (10:3-4), which are the seventh through eleventh items of Christ's riches in 1 Corinthians. Truly, the Lord is rich to all who call upon Him. By calling, "O Lord Jesus," we enjoy Him as the power and wisdom of God, as our righteousness, sanctification, and redemption, and as the deep things of God, the foundation, the Passover, and our spiritual food, spiritual drink, and spiritual rock. Moreover, the way to partake of all these riches of Christ is to call on His name.

CHRIST BEING THE HEAD, THE FIRSTFRUITS, THE SECOND MAN, THE LAST ADAM, THE LIFE-GIVING SPIRIT, THE BODY, AND THE BODY-CHRIST

After this group of eleven items of what Christ is, there are another seven items. Christ is the Head of every man (11:3a), the firstfruits (15:20, 23), the second man (v. 47b), the last Adam, and the life-giving Spirit (v. 45b). Since Christ is the first, the second, and the last, He is everything, and He is every member of the Body. As our everything, He takes our position; that is, He is everything, and we are nothing. However, we have all been put into Him. We are nothing in ourselves, but we have everything in Him. We may never have dreamed that Christ is so much. Moreover, Christ is not only the Head but also the Body. Verse 12 of chapter 12 says, "Even as the body is one and has many members, yet all the members of the body, being many, are one body, so also is the Christ." Most Christians realize that Christ is the Head, but they do not consider that He is also the Body. According to the concept we received from Christianity, we consider that Christ is the Head and that the church is the Body. Strictly speaking, however, this is a wrong concept. It is wrong to say that a man's head is the man himself but that his body is someone else. A man is a whole person, including his head and his body. Likewise, Christ is a complete person, both the Head and the Body.

Since Christ is both the Head and the Body, He is the Body-Christ. This simply means that He is no longer only the individual Christ; He is also the corporate Christ. Christ has an individual aspect and a corporate aspect. Individually, He is Christ, and corporately, He is the Body-Christ. On the Lord's table there are the bread and the cup. The bread signifies Christ's body in two aspects. First, it signifies the physical body of Jesus, in which He was pierced, crucified on the cross, and shed His blood for us, and second, it signifies the mystical Body of Christ. The mystical Body of Christ is the corporate Christ, the Body-Christ. When we partake of the bread at the Lord's table, we are eating not only the individual Christ but also the corporate Christ. We enjoy the mystical Body of Christ, and we participate in the Body-Christ.

THE PROPER CHURCH LIFE ISSUING FROM OUR ENJOYMENT OF CHRIST BY CALLING ON HIS NAME

As we have seen, 1 Corinthians tells us that we need to enjoy and partake of all the riches of Christ by calling, "O Lord Jesus." In this way He becomes our power, wisdom, righteousness, sanctification, redemption, the deep things of God, the foundation, the Passover, our spiritual food, spiritual drink, and spiritual rock, the Head, the firstfruits, the second man, the last Adam, the life-giving Spirit, the Body, and the Body-Christ. The issue of this enjoyment of Christ is the church life. The way to have the church life is not to receive doctrinal teachings and be corrected and adjusted in the way of organization. Organizing can produce a society, but it can never produce the Body. The Body comes out of the enjoyment of Christ. By our calling on this rich Christ, on the Lord who is rich to all, He enters into us, and we digest and assimilate Him so that He comes into every part of our being to be our organic element, even to become us. Books on nutrition tell us that we are what we eat. If we eat fish and chicken every day, we will eventually be constituted with fish and chicken. In the same way, if we eat Jesus, we will eventually become Him. Paul says, "To me, to live is Christ" (Phil. 1:21). To us, to live is

Christ, because we eat Christ day by day and hour after hour. Eventually, we all become Christ. Since there is only one Jesus, the more we eat Jesus and become Him, the more we will be in oneness. In the church we are enjoying not only the individual Christ but also the corporate Christ, the Body-Christ.

THE TOP ENJOYMENT OF CHRIST BEING THE ENJOYMENT OF THE CORPORATE CHRIST, THE BODY-CHRIST

Many Christians may feel that the Sunday morning service is too poor and that because of this it is more profitable to stay home and study a good reference Bible with concordances, word studies, and notes. This is not bad; it is better than nothing. However, whoever does this will not receive as much enjoyment of the Lord as he could receive in a meeting of the church. Regardless of how much we enjoy Jesus in our personal study of the Bible, we still cannot enjoy the corporate Christ in this way. In order to enjoy the corporate Christ, the Body-Christ, we need to come to the church meetings. We must be in the Body in a practical way. First Corinthians 12:13 says, "For also in one Spirit we were all baptized into one Body, whether Jews or Greeks, whether slaves or free, and were all given to drink one Spirit." To be given to drink is to be positioned to drink, which, according to the whole verse, is to be put into the Body. If we stay away from the meetings yet still try to pray-read, call on the Lord, and even shout, we will have a certain amount of enjoyment, but this enjoyment will be restricted and limited. It is difficult to make a fire with only one piece of wood. It is better to have many pieces. Then one piece will burn another. When one person says, "O Lord," another says, "Hallelujah," and a third person says, "Amen," we burn one another. We strengthen, minister to, and supply one another. In this way we enjoy not only the Head but the Head with the Body, and not only the individual Christ but the corporate Christ, the Body-Christ.

First, verse 12 tells us that just as the body has many members but is one body, so also is the Christ. Then verse 13 begins with the word *for*, indicating that it is a continuation, definition, and explanation of the foregoing verse. All the members are one Body, and this Body is Christ, because in one Spirit we were all baptized into one Body. As we pointed out before, without our spirit our body would be a corpse. When the spirit leaves the body, the body decomposes. However, with our spirit still in our body, the many members of our body are living and are one. It is our spirit that keeps all the members joined as one. In the same way, we as the many members of the Body of Christ are one because we have been baptized in the Spirit. Moreover, the one Spirit in whom we have been baptized is Christ, who became the life-giving Spirit. Therefore, the Body is Christ, and Christ is the Body.

We have all been positioned in the Body to drink of the one Spirit. Again, this one Spirit is the life-giving Spirit, which is Christ. We have been put into Christ, the life-giving Spirit, and we have been positioned in the Body. Now, since we are in the Body, we need to drink this one Spirit, which is Christ. Eventually we are filled, flooded, saturated, and permeated by the Spirit. Therefore, we are one with one another and with Christ as one Body, which is Christ Himself.

When we enjoy Christ, we enjoy the Body, including all the members. For more than forty years I have been continually enjoying the Body-Christ in a corporate way. Without the Body, I could try to declare that Christ is rich, but eventually I would no longer be able to speak. When I am with the Body, however, the more I speak, the more I have something to speak. This is because the more my speaking supplies the Body, the more I am supplied by the Body. While I am ministering to the Body, the Body is ministering to me. If the saints were to listen to my speaking without responding, the supply of the Body would be cut off from me, and I would not be able to speak. Without the supply of the Body, I have nothing with which to supply the Body. On the other hand, if while I am speaking, all the members are responding, the Body is ministering to me. Then there is a current, a circulation, in the Body-Christ. Today we are enjoying the Body-Christ.

Many good teachers have pointed out that in 1 Corinthians Christ is power, wisdom, righteousness, sanctification, redemption, the deep things of God, the foundation, our Passover, our spiritual food, spiritual drink, and spiritual rock, and the Head. However, most teachers would not tell us that Christ is the life-giving Spirit or that He is the Body-Christ. We are enjoying Christ all the way from the power and wisdom of God to the firstfruits, the second man, the last Adam, the life-giving Spirit, and the Body. Moreover, the issue of the enjoyment of all the items of Christ is the Body-Christ. The Body-Christ comes out of the full enjoyment of the riches of Christ. To enjoy Christ as the power of God is wonderful, but it cannot compare with the enjoyment of Christ as the Body-Christ. To enjoy Christ as power is to enjoy Him in one aspect, but to enjoy Him as the Body-Christ is to enjoy Him in fullness.

Our enjoyment of the Body-Christ is the reason we sing, "We come together—there's nothing better" (*Hymns*, #1196). Coming together as the Body-Christ is better than waiting for a heaven that is far away and in the future. In the church we come together here and now. There is nothing better than this, because nowhere else can we enjoy the Body-Christ. If we stay at home, we may be able to enjoy Christ as our power, wisdom, or other items, but in order to enjoy the Body-Christ, we must be in the church. We may miss many other things, but we should not miss one meeting of the church. It is in the church that we are in the position to drink the Body-Christ, the Christ who is the life-giving Spirit in the Body. There is no other place to drink the Body-Christ but in the coming together of the church. Even in the meetings of the local churches we do not enjoy Christ as much as we do in the conferences of the churches. In the conference meetings we enjoy an even greater Body-Christ. Therefore, it is worthwhile to pay the price to come to the conferences. We cannot obtain such an enjoyment anywhere else. Hallelujah, in the church we enjoy the Body-Christ!

CHAPTER FOUR

COMING BACK TO
THE PROPER GROUND OF ONENESS
AND FELLOWSHIPPING TO ENJOY
THE BODY-CHRIST

Scripture Reading: 1 Cor. 1:2, 10-13a; 3:3-4; 12:18-27

God's purpose is to have the Body of Christ. Ephesians 4:4 through 6 says, "One Body and one Spirit...one Lord...one God and Father of all." The Triune God was consummated to be the Spirit for the Body. As we saw in the previous chapter, this Spirit, who is Christ Himself, becomes the Body-Christ (2 Cor. 3:17; 1 Cor. 15:45b; 12:12-13).

GOD PRESENTING HIMSELF TO US IN CHRIST
IN THE FORM OF FOOD

According to the clear revelation of the Bible, the Father is in the Son. In John 14 Philip asked the Lord Jesus, "Lord, show us the Father and it is sufficient for us." The Lord replied, "Have I been so long a time with you, and you have not known Me, Philip? He who has seen Me has seen the Father; how is it that you say, Show us the Father? Do you not believe that I am in the Father and the Father is in Me?" (vv. 8-10a). According to the Lord's word to Philip, whoever sees the Son sees the Father also, because the Father is in the Son, and the Son is in the Father. Moreover, the Son today is the life-giving Spirit. Therefore, the life-giving Spirit is the Triune God.

It is impossible for us to understand the mystery of the Triune God. Even we ourselves are a mystery. We all know that we have a body, but we also have a spirit and a soul (1 Thes. 5:23). We even have two hearts, a physical heart and a psychological heart. Our physical heart may be sound and healthy, but our psychological heart is corrupt, rotten, and incurable. Jeremiah 17:9 says, "The heart is deceitful above all things, / And it is incurable; / Who can know it?" We know where our physical heart is, but no one can locate our psychological heart—our soul with our mind, emotion, and will, plus our conscience—and no one can see our spirit. It is impossible to systemize all the wonderful, inward parts of our being.

In the Lord's recovery we do not stress theological knowledge; rather, we stress the enjoyment of the Lord by our eating Him. Many theologians are foolish, thinking that they can understand the Triune God. The more books they publish to define Him, the more confusion they cause. If we cannot understand a small mystery such as ourselves, how can we understand the Triune God? We cannot even understand the food we eat. We may not know the elements in various kinds of foods, but we know that we can receive these elements by eating and drinking the food. In the same way, the Triune God is not for our understanding. He is for our eating. Jesus said, "I am the bread of life," and "He who eats Me, he also shall live because of Me" (John 6:35a, 57b). After God created man, He did not set up a seminary and charge Adam and Eve to diligently study the doctrines related to God. Instead, God planted a garden. We all know that a garden is for growing things to eat. Genesis 2:9 tells us that in the garden God caused to grow every tree that is pleasant to the sight and good for food. Nothing in the garden was good for teaching; everything was good for food. Moreover, in the middle of the garden was the tree of life. Eventually, God Himself came in the flesh, presenting Himself to His creatures and saying, "I am the bread of life." This means that the tree of life is simply Jesus, who is God Himself coming in the flesh to present Himself to man in the form of food.

Even today God does not present Himself mainly as the almighty One, commanding us to prostrate before Him and worship. Rather, in presenting Himself to us, God makes Himself small. Whatever we eat is much smaller than we are. If something is bigger than we are, we cannot eat it. God does not come to us mainly as the One who is greater than we are.

He comes to present Himself as food, as a small loaf, the bread of life. By so doing, God indicates that He wants us to eat Him. A popular hymn in Christianity says, "How great Thou art." However, we all need to praise Him by saying, "How small Thou art." He is small enough for us to eat. At the beginning of the Bible there is the tree of life, and at the end of the Bible is the final promise: "Blessed are those who wash their robes that they may have right to the tree of life" (Rev. 22:14). The tree of life is God Himself as our food. We all need to realize that the Triune God is good for food.

EATING THE TRIUNE GOD ISSUING IN THE CHURCH, THE BODY OF CHRIST

We also must see that when we eat the Triune God, there is a wonderful result, which is the church, the Body of Christ. The Body is the issue of our eating the Triune God. The more we say, "O Lord Jesus," the more we take the Lord into us, and the more we take Him in, the more He becomes us and we become Him. We are what we eat. As we eat Jesus, we are becoming Jesus in a corporate way. This corporate Jesus is the Body of Christ. The Body-Christ comes out of our eating the Triune God.

It is true that we need to understand the Bible, but the enemy, Satan, has subtly deceived many Christians into thinking that the Bible is only for teaching and understanding. Jesus told the devil, "Man shall not live on bread alone, but on every word that proceeds out through the mouth of God" (Matt. 4:4). This proves that, strictly speaking, the Bible is not for teaching but for nourishing. We should read the Bible not only to study it; we need to eat the word of the Bible. Jeremiah proclaimed, "Your words were found and I ate them" (Jer. 15:16). It is true that the Bible is the revelation of God, but again the enemy uses this concept in a subtle way. The Bible is not only the revelation of God but also the breath of God, as is confirmed by Paul's word in 2 Timothy 3:16: "All Scripture is God-breathed." The Bible is the breathing out of God Himself. What He breathes out, we must breathe in.

The principle of eating is simply to take something that is

outside of us into our being, digest it, and assimilate it into our organic tissues to make it our own element. To eat God, therefore, is to take God into our being and assimilate what He is into our basic structure, our organic inner being, to make us what He is. God can be assimilated into our being. We need to tell people the wonderful fact that as human beings who have eaten, digested, and assimilated the Triune God, we now have the divine element. Moreover, since we have the divine element in a corporate way, we are the Body-Christ. The proper church life, the Body-Christ, comes out of our eating the Triune God. This is a wonderful and marvelous matter. This is God's intention, desire, and eternal purpose (Eph. 3:9-11). How subtle the enemy of God is! The old serpent has crept in deceitfully to deaden the living of the believers and cause divisions through differing teachings and opinions. This is why in today's Christianity we do not see the Body-Christ, the corporate Jesus. Instead, what we see are many divisions.

COMING BACK TO THE PROPER GROUND
OF THE ONENESS OF THE CHURCH

Some may say that they are not in division because they are no longer in the denominations. To give up the denominations is a good beginning, but it is still short. We must come all the way back to the proper ground of the church. We may illustrate this with the typology of the Old Testament. At the time Solomon built the temple in the good land, all the children of Israel were one. Because of their degradation, however, some of them were carried away into Syria, some into Egypt, and some into Babylon. They all were scattered. Instead of being one, they became several divisions. Many years later, God commanded them to return to the good land. After becoming clear that Babylon was not the right place to be, many came out of Babylon. However, some might have stopped midway between Babylon and Jerusalem, some in one place and some in another. Eventually, the result was that there were more divisions. At first there were only a few large divisions, but after many left Babylon, they became many smaller divisions.

Some, however, received the vision not only of leaving Babylon but of coming back to Jerusalem, and many eventually did come back. In Babylon there might have been a kind of oneness, a oneness in division, a subtle, divisive "oneness," but Jerusalem was the place of the proper oneness (Deut. 12:5-18; 2 Chron. 6:5-6; John 4:20). This is a picture of the many non-denominational groups. There is no oneness among the many free groups. The proper oneness is the oneness of the church on the proper ground. Those who have come out of the denominations are happy to be nondenominational. On the one hand, it is good not to call oneself a Baptist, Lutheran, Methodist, Presbyterian, Episcopalian, or Catholic. On the other hand, God has no intention that we be a part of nothing and remain "midway." In this sense, we must be neither denominational nor nondenominational, because God's intention is to have the Body. Satan in his subtlety has damaged the Body, but God is coming in today to carry out His recovery. He is demanding that all His seekers and lovers leave Babylon, not remain midway, and come back to the ground of oneness, the spiritual Jerusalem.

By this we can see that there are two different kinds of oneness—the oneness in Babylon and the oneness in Jerusalem. However, only the oneness in Jerusalem is the proper oneness. Although many of the children of Israel remained in Babylon, they were not the nation of Israel. The nation of Israel was in the good land. When those who returned to the good land stood on the ground of oneness to declare that they were the nation of Israel, some in Babylon might have been unhappy. They might have said, "Are only you the nation of Israel? Are we not Israel also? We are all brothers. We all have the same Jewish life and are of the same Jewish blood. How can you say that you are the nation of Israel and that we are not?" The same condition exists today among the Jews. There are nearly thirteen million Jews on the earth today, and over one million are in New York City alone. Only a few million, however, have returned to Palestine. It is only this small number that are recognized as the nation of Israel. Concerning those who return to the proper ground, the number is not the most important factor (cf. Ezra 2:64-65).

What matters is the ground of oneness. Those Jews in New York are real Jews, and they may give much money for the nation of Israel. However, they are not the nation of Israel, because they are not on the proper ground. If they want to be in the nation of Israel, they must return to the land of Israel.

It is the same with the Lord's recovery today. When we say that we are the church, many in the denominations are offended. Thousands of them may be genuine Christians, children of God. They may love the Lord, love the Bible, and love people's souls, and they may do a certain amount of work for the Lord. However, they still say that they are Lutheran, Presbyterian, or something else. Since they do this, they lose the proper ground. They are the right persons, but their position is wrong. They need to come back to the real Jerusalem, the proper ground of oneness. All the Jews in the world today are privileged to return to Israel. Because they have Jewish blood, they will be received into the nation of Israel. Likewise, as believers we have the proper birth; however, most Christians have the wrong position. As long as they keep their old position in Babylon or at a midway point, they miss the proper ground of the church. They are right persons on the wrong ground. We must all give up the wrong ground and return to the proper ground of oneness. We must stress this, because today we are under a situation of confusion. God's intention is that we would be a corporate Body in oneness.

We need to know which meeting of Christians is on the proper ground of oneness. There are many Christian organizations, groups, and "bodies" today. Again, we may compare them to the Jews. Among the Jews today there are many organizations formed to help the nation of Israel. Among all these gatherings of Jews, however, only that group in Palestine is on the proper ground. If all the Jews in Israel were in New York, they would no longer be the nation of Israel. They would lose the ground. Likewise, if those in the Jewish organizations would return to Palestine, they would become the nation of Israel. It is not the number that is important; it is the proper ground. If we remain in Babylon or midway in the free groups, we are not the church. We may be members of Christ's Body, but we lose the ground to be the church in practicality. We all need to come back to the proper ground of the genuine oneness, not the "oneness" in the divisions.

LIVING A LIFE OF ONENESS IN THE CHURCH

Putting Our Trust in the Lord and Having No Choice of Our Own

On the one hand, it is wonderful to come together in oneness. On the other hand, however, it is difficult to come together. Even for two brothers to live together in the same room is a hardship. One may want the windows closed, and the other may want them open. Since the church life is a life of togetherness, what can we do? We must all put our trust in the Lord. The two brothers can say, "Lord, if You put us together, we have no choice. We cannot choose to have the windows open or shut. Lord, it is up to You." To keep the windows open or shut does not matter. We must learn the lesson of not having any choice and of leaving everything up to the Lord.

Having No Confidence in Ourselves but Doing All Things by the Body

Moreover, in our life of togetherness we should not do things by ourselves or have any confidence in ourselves. We must not say, "I am very clear. I checked with the Bible, and what I am doing is fully scriptural. I prayed that the Lord would give me signs, and I received several. Now I am clear that what I am planning to do is of the Lord. Acts 5:29 says that it is necessary to obey God rather than men. Do not pressure me; let me go. You are merely men, and I must obey God." If anyone holds this attitude, he is deceived.

The church life is the Body life. If our body remains in the United States, our hand cannot say, "I am clear to go to Taiwan. I must obey this feeling and not the body." In principle, this is what some of us have done in the past. If the Body does not share our feeling, we should say, "Praise the Lord, I am enjoying the Body-Christ, not an individual Christ." If we do this, we will be safeguarded. The Body is a real safeguard to us. In the past I sometimes felt that the brothers were too slow to understand the Lord's will and that as long as I was clear, I could go on without them. Eventually, however, I realized that this was wrong. This is to be individualistic and not to care for the Body. We all need to learn the lesson. We should never do things in the church life in an individualistic way. We must always be checked by the Body. Whatever the Body says is better, and if the Body does not agree, we should not go ahead. Then the Body will be our safeguard. As long as we take care of the Body, we are fully protected.

Not Dealing with Others to Correct or Adjust Them, but Ministering the Life Supply through Fellowship

In the church life we should also avoid dealing with others in the way of correcting or adjusting them. If we realize that some brothers are wrong in some matter, we may think that we have a burden from the Lord to charge them to repent and change their attitude and way. This never works. What we have in our physical body is simply the circulation of blood. The "circulation" in the Body of Christ is fellowship, not dealing. If we feel that some brothers are wrong and are even causing a loss to the Body, we should not go to them to deal with them. We should pray to the Lord again and again. Then we may have the deep sensation from the Lord to fellowship with some other brothers, pray for the needy ones, and seek the Lord's leading together. Eventually, we may contact the ones who are wrong. At this time we should not touch their mistakes. We need to leave their mistakes to the Lord. Then after several contacts, we can fellowship with them about the needs. This is to keep the circulation of blood in the Body. The circulation of blood carries nourishment, and within this nourishment are the elements that spontaneously kill and discharge the germs. Perhaps after several times of fellowship, they may mention their problem to us. At that time we still should not touch their problem too much. We should only say a little, ministering life to them on the positive side. We may not even know at what point the disease is healed. Simply by our fellowship we bring the circulation of life again and again until the problem is gone. Then they may testify, "Praise the Lord! Our problem is gone and under the Lord's blood." Death will be swallowed up by life even if we never talk to them about their mistakes. To deal with people never works. What we always need in the church life is fellowship, the circulation of life.

After a short time in the church life, a young brother may still have his old, improper appearance. We should not go to tell him, "Brother, you need to know that in the church we should not look like this." This is to deal with him in a wrong way. Rather, we should pick up a burden for that brother and go to him with one or two others for the purpose of fellowship. While we are fellowshipping with him, the Holy Spirit, the life within, will speak to him. Then after we leave, he may go to adjust his appearance, and in the next meeting we will see a new shining face. We may be surprised at the Lord's transforming work in this brother. The brother will not have a mere outward correction. He will have transformation out of the life supply he received through our fellowship. If we deal with a new one wrongly, we will damage the Lord's work. We should simply pick up the burden to fellowship with that one.

All the Members Functioning
to Fellowship in Life and by Love

The denominations in Christianity depend on one or a few pastors, but in the Lord's Body we do not need that kind of pastor. Instead, we need the fellowship of all the members. All the members are the promoters, not of correction but of the circulation of life. As long as life circulates among us, it will regulate, transform, and shape us. Therefore, we should not go to people to correct them. We must put our trust in the fellowship of life. We should always go to our fellow members to fellowship with them in life by love. This is a daily work. Day after day we will see the growth, transformation, and wonderful change in all the saints. In this way we will remain on the proper ground of oneness with the necessary fellowship to enjoy the Body-Christ. This is the proper way to have the church life.

Never Gossiping but
Treasuring the Precious Body Life

We must also never gossip or spread any negative word. Even if we see the shortages or weakness of a certain brother or sister, we can tell it to the Lord, but we should never speak it to anyone else. We need to pray for the members. Any kind of gossip only spreads death in the Body. Gossip is a spreading of germs to kill the Body. We must treasure the fact that we are in the Body life. The Body life should be so precious to us that we would not do anything to damage it. If we see some weak points in one another, we should bring the situation to the Lord, pray, and seek the Lord's leading to go to fellowship with the involved parties, not to point out their weaknesses but to minister life so that the life supply will swallow up the weaknesses. This is the proper way to preserve the church life. We must be on the proper ground, and we must fellowship again and again. Then we will enjoy the Body-Christ.

ABOUT THE AUTHOR

Witness Lee was born in 1905 in northern China and raised in a Christian family. At age 19 he was fully captured for Christ and immediately consecrated himself to preach the gospel for the rest of his life. Early in his service, he met Watchman Nee, a renowned preacher, teacher, and writer. Witness Lee labored together with Watchman Nee under his direction. In 1934 Watchman Nee entrusted Witness Lee with the responsibility for his publication operation, called the Shanghai Gospel Bookroom.

Prior to the Communist takeover in 1949, Witness Lee was sent by Watchman Nee and his other co-workers to Taiwan to ensure that the things delivered to them by the Lord would not be lost. Watchman Nee instructed Witness Lee to continue the former's publishing operation abroad as the Taiwan Gospel Bookroom, which has been publicly recognized as the publisher of Watchman Nee's works outside China. Witness Lee's work in Taiwan manifested the Lord's abundant blessing. From a mere 350 believers, newly fled from the mainland, the churches in Taiwan grew to 20,000 in five years.

In 1962 Witness Lee felt led of the Lord to come to the United States, settling in California. During his 35 years of service in the U.S., he ministered in weekly meetings and weekend conferences, delivering several thousand spoken messages. Much of his speaking has since been published as over 400 titles. Many of these have been translated into over fourteen languages. He gave his last public conference in February 1997 at the age of 91.

He leaves behind a prolific presentation of the truth in the Bible. His major work, *Life-study of the Bible,* comprises over 25,000 pages of commentary on every book of the Bible from the perspective of the believers' enjoyment and experience of God's divine life in Christ through the Holy Spirit. Witness Lee was the chief editor of a new translation of the New Testament into Chinese called the Recovery Version and directed the translation of the same into English. The Recovery Version also appears in a number of other languages. He provided an extensive body of footnotes, outlines, and spiritual cross references. A radio broadcast of his messages can be heard on Christian radio stations in the United States. In 1965 Witness Lee founded Living Stream Ministry, a non-profit corporation, located in Anaheim, California, which officially presents his and Watchman Nee's ministry.

Witness Lee's ministry emphasizes the experience of Christ as life and the practical oneness of the believers as the Body of Christ. Stressing the importance of attending to both these matters, he led the churches under his care to grow in Christian life and function. He was unbending in his conviction that God's goal is not narrow sectarianism but the Body of Christ. In time, believers began to meet simply as the church in their localities in response to this conviction. In recent years a number of new churches have been raised up in Russia and in many eastern European countries.

OTHER BOOKS PUBLISHED BY
Living Stream Ministry

Titles by Witness Lee:

Abraham—Called by God	0-7363-0359-6
The Experience of Life	0-87083-417-7
The Knowledge of Life	0-87083-419-3
The Tree of Life	0-87083-300-6
The Economy of God	0-87083-415-0
The Divine Economy	0-87083-268-9
God's New Testament Economy	0-87083-199-2
The World Situation and God's Move	0-87083-092-9
Christ vs. Religion	0-87083-010-4
The All-inclusive Christ	0-87083-020-1
Gospel Outlines	0-87083-039-2
Character	0-87083-322-7
The Secret of Experiencing Christ	0-87083-227-1
The Life and Way for the Practice of the Church Life	0-87083-785-0
The Basic Revelation in the Holy Scriptures	0-87083-105-4
The Crucial Revelation of Life in the Scriptures	0-87083-372-3
The Spirit with Our Spirit	0-87083-798-2
Christ as the Reality	0-87083-047-3
The Central Line of the Divine Revelation	0-87083-960-8
The Full Knowledge of the Word of God	0-87083-289-1
Watchman Nee—A Seer of the Divine Revelation ...	0-87083-625-0

Titles by Watchman Nee:

How to Study the Bible	0-7363-0407-X
God's Overcomers	0-7363-0433-9
The New Covenant	0-7363-0088-0
The Spiritual Man 3 volumes	0-7363-0269-7
Authority and Submission	0-7363-0185-2
The Overcoming Life	1-57593-817-0
The Glorious Church	0-87083-745-1
The Prayer Ministry of the Church	0-87083-860-1
The Breaking of the Outer Man and the Release ...	1-57593-955-X
The Mystery of Christ	1-57593-954-1
The God of Abraham, Isaac, and Jacob	0-87083-932-2
The Song of Songs	0-87083-872-5
The Gospel of God 2 volumes	1-57593-953-3
The Normal Christian Church Life	0-87083-027-9
The Character of the Lord's Worker	1-57593-322-5
The Normal Christian Faith	0-87083-748-6
Watchman Nee's Testimony	0-87083-051-1

Available at
Christian bookstores, or contact Living Stream Ministry
2431 W. La Palma Ave. • Anaheim, CA 92801
1-800-549-5164 • www.livingstream.com